a

is

for

airport

b
is
for
baseball

allan moak

tundra books

a
big
city
abc

© 1984, Allan Moak

Published in Canada by Tundra Books, Montreal, Quebec H3G 1R4

Published in the United States by Tundra Books of Northern New York, Plattsburgh, N.Y. 12901

Hardcover ISBN 0-88776-161-5

Paperback ISBN 0-88776-238-7

Canadian Cataloguing in Publication Data

Moak, Allan
  A big city ABC

ISBN 0-88776-161-5 (bound) –
ISBN 0-88776-238-7 (pbk.)

  1. English language – Alphabet – Juvenile literature.
2. Toronto (Ont.) – Juvenile literature.   I. Title.

PE1155.M62 1984   j421'.1   C84-9869-3 rev.

Printed in Hong Kong by South China Printing Company (1988) Limited.

C
is
for
castle

d

is

for

deli

e
is
for
exca-
vation

f

is

for

fire-

works

g

is

for

green-

house

h

is

for

horses

i
is
for
island
ferry

j

is

for

junk

store

k

is

for

kites

I

is

for

life-

guard

m

is

for

market

n

is

for

neigh-

bour-

hood

O is for

october

p

is

for

park

q

is

for

queen

r

is

for

rink

ALLAN MOAK

S

is

for

science

centre

t

is

for

tug-

boat

u
is
for
mbrella

V

is

for

variety

store

W

is

for

winter

X
is
for
The EX

y

is

for

yule-

tide

Z

is

for

zoo

oronto

Toronto, Canada's largest city and one of the great cities of the world, means different things to different people. For some it is the business centre of the country with its soaring office towers and banks. For others it is the arts capital with galleries, theatres, radio and television studios. I see it through children's eyes, and my Toronto is for children. It was not hard, for many of the things that kids most like in this great city, I still like too.

Airport: It is now called the Lester B. Pearson International Airport, but many people in Toronto still think of it as the Toronto International Airport or Malton Airport. Even when they are not taking a plane, children like to go out to the two terminal buildings to watch the huge airliners arriving or taking off every few seconds on flights across Canada and to places all over the world.

Baseball: Exhibition Stadium in the Canadian National Exhibition grounds is home for the Toronto Blue Jays. At afternoon games, children make up a large number of the 50,000 fans. I painted the Jays playing the Red Sox. Will it be a home run? Can you find the Jays' mascot, B.J. Bird, in the painting?

Castle: Casa Loma stands high on a hill overlooking mid-town Toronto. Sir Henry Mill Pellatt's 98-room medieval castle was completed in 1913, and its huge towers and secret passages have made it a fairy-tale place for children ever since. After a big snowfall, the castle looks even more beautiful.

Deli: Next to painting, I think eating is the most fun. Toronto has some of the finest delis anywhere and I love to go into them. The smells that greet one seem to bring the world into one small place: spicy sausages, sweet pastries, pickles, cheeses — even bird's-nest soup.

Excavation: It is no use my telling you where I painted this huge hole in the earth in downtown Toronto because by the time you read this, it won't be there. In the 20 years I have lived in Toronto, I feel the city has been rebuilt before my eyes. Can **you** walk past a construction site without stopping to watch? Don't the earth movers remind you of toys in a sandbox?

Fireworks: The Chinese invented fireworks, so I chose China Court on Spadina Avenue, south of Dundas Street, as the setting for this painting. It was built by craftsmen brought from Hong Kong and its colourful pagodas and bridges remain a centre of Toronto's Chinese community.

Greenhouse: Allan Gardens at Sherbourne and Carlton Streets was developed in 1909 in the Victorian style. It is a tropical paradise of plants and flowers. Particularly in winter when the city's outdoor gardens are asleep, Allan Gardens is a great place to visit. The greenhouse and park around it cover a whole city block.

Horses: The circus usually comes to Toronto during February. When the show is set up at the Maple Leaf Gardens on Carlton at Church Street, we are all children together as we watch the exciting acts. I like the horses and bareback riders best. That's why I painted them.

Island Ferry: The ferryboat *Sam McBride* was named after a Toronto mayor who first took office in 1928. It crosses the harbour to the Toronto Islands: Ward's, Hanlan's and Centre Island, where we can all go as families for picnics. Centre Island is a fine spot for watching birds and people and each summer Torontonians from the Caribbean stage their Caribana festival with bright costumes, fun music and dancing.

Junk Store: I love to collect junk, so painting this shop on Queen Street West was great fun for me. Old toys, old machinery, old anything — if I keep any of it long enough, it might be called "antique." Toronto is one of the few big cities to still have streetcars, so I put one of our new ones in the background. Have you ever ridden on a bright red streetcar?

Kites: Every summer in Toronto, kites fly in our parks and open spaces. The old lighthouse in this painting was moved from its original site to Lakeshore Boulevard near the Princes' Gates of the Canadian National Exhibition. Here on the harbour front where the breezes are light and airy, seagulls join the kites in the clear blue sky.

Lifeguard: A summer's day on the beach wouldn't be complete without a swim and ice cream. The Eastern Beaches Park covers the entire waterfront from Ashbridges Bay to the eastern city lights. Here I painted Kew Beach with its boardwalk and bicycle path. The lifeguard keeps a lookout for emergencies in the water.

Market: Children don't always like going shopping for food but Kensington Market near College Street and Spadina Avenue offers so much to look at, hear and smell that a visit there is like a little trip around the world. It used to be known as the Jewish market, but today nearly every immigrant group is well represented, particularly the Portuguese.

Neighbourhood: The narrow back laneways of west Toronto are wonderful play areas for children. Hockey is often practised in them all the year round. This painting was inspired by the lane behind a house I used to live in on Palmerston Boulevard.

October: I wanted to include an autumn scene in this book. The fun of playing in the leaves is a special Toronto treat. We are lucky to have so many trees that our town has actually been called the "City of Trees." The house in the painting is where I now live on Westmoreland Avenue.

Park: Toronto has about 330 parks and "parkettes," covering 650 hectares. On a summer day the wading pools are asplash with kids keeping cool, and the ice cream trucks with their bells jingling are never far away. This park is near Palmerston Boulevard and Ulster Street.

Queen: Toronto is often called the Queen City, and reminders of Queen Victoria are everywhere. Her monument stands in front of the Legislative Buildings in Queen's Park where the Provincial Parliament of Ontario meets. The brownstone and granite buildings were designed by architect R.A. Waite and opened in 1893.

Rink: Can any other city in the world boast a skating rink for children and parents right in front of its city hall? And what a place to skate! One of the world's most admired buildings, it was designed by Finnish architect Viljo Revell and opened in 1965. Situated in Nathan Phillips Square, it is a lasting monument to one of Toronto's most innovative mayors. The sculpture called *The Archer* is by a famous British artist, Henry Moore.

Science Centre: The Ontario Science Centre at Don Mills Road and Eglinton Avenue East is a busy, exciting place to visit. Kids can play astronaut on a simulated space flight, try papermaking, test their reaction time or take part in a static electricity demonstration. I have shown part of Rowland Emett's Magical Machines called "The Afternoon Tea-Train to Wisteria Halt."

Tugboat: This old steam-powered tugboat, the *Ned Hanlan*, named in honour of a famous Toronto athlete, served for many years in the Toronto harbour. It was retired, restored and placed on permanent display at the Canadian National Exhibition grounds next to the Marine Museum.

Umbrella: Now and then it rains in Toronto, and when umbrellas go up they make very colourful patterns on the streets. I chose Parliament Street as the background because it has architecture that recalls Toronto's earlier years. That's the spire of St. James Cathedral in the background.

Variety Store: Every neighbourhood has its favourite variety store, as popular with the children as with their moms and dads. This one is on Dovercourt Road at the corner of Shanly Street. Have you a favourite?

Winter: When Toronto gets a big snowfall, it becomes a city where children blossom like flowers. Or arrive like armies? Snow forts are built, snowballs are thrown. Quieter youngsters are happy to build snowmen or, in this case, a snow angel in this westend back lane.

The Ex: Even though it doesn't start with the letter X, it sounds like it. The Canadian National Exhibition is held the last three weeks of August and it has Canada's largest and most exciting midway — along with exhibits from around the world. Children look forward to the Ex like Christmas, and older Torontonians remember it as one of the happiest places of their own childhood. The Exhibition Park on a 150 hectare site on the shores of Lake Ontario also has a great agricultural "winter" fair held every autumn.

Yuletide: Around Christmas time each year, Toronto lights up like a tree as we decorate our homes to welcome the wonderful season. These houses are on Mutual Street in the downtown area. Sometimes we're lucky and we have a white Christmas.

Zoo: The Metro Toronto Zoo on Meadowvale Road north of Highway 401 is one of the largest in the world with 290 hectares and 3,500 animals. It was just too large for one painting, so I composed a fanciful zoo with children painting the animals and placed it in the harbourfront area with the Ontario Place Cinesphere and the C.N. Tower in the background.

And now, make up and paint A BIG CITY ABC of your own favourite places!

allan moak

Allan Moak has lived and painted in Toronto for 20 years. His charming works, filled with detail and colour, have been exhibited in some 25 galleries across Canada and are in private collections throughout North America.

He was born and grew up in Kingston, Ontario, and began painting while still a very young teenager. His first studio was in a loft over a sailmaker's shop and he used the scraps of discarded sailcloth as canvas to paint on. Entirely self-taught, he has always painted the world around him with the freedom and delight of a primitive painter — or of a child.

It was not difficult for him to see Toronto through the eyes of children because he has always observed life that way. Also, he confesses to still liking to do many of the things children like: kite flying, making things with wood, reading scary ghost stories and trying things out at the Ontario Science Centre. To create A BIG CITY ABC, he simply chose some of the places he feels make Toronto a particularly wonderful city for children. His project was chosen for special assistance by the Toronto Sesquicentennial Publications Committee.